staying strong

a journal

Demi Lovato

Feiwel and Friends
NEW YORK

A FEIWEL AND FRIENDS BOOK
An Imprint of Macmillan

Feiwel and Friends books may be purchased for business or promotional use.
For information on bulk purchases, please contact the Macmillan Corporate
and Premium Sales Department at (800) 221-7945 x5442 or by e-mail
at specialmarkets@macmillan.com.

Library of Congress Cataloging-in-Publication Data Available

ISBN: 978-1-250-06352-6

Book design by April Ward

Feiwel and Friends logo designed by Filomena Tuosto

First Edition: 2014

2   4   6   8   10   9   7   5   3   1

*O*ne of the most important things I've learned on my journey is the importance of channeling my emotions and expressing myself, which everyone does differently. I like to read affirmations, set goals for myself on a daily basis, and I like to journal.

Journaling is a purifying experience—it takes its shape in so many forms. Whether I'm writing poems or song lyrics, drawing or doodling, or simply copying down favorite quotes or passages, this form of self-expression helps release the pain and the fear, or any emotions, really. It sheds light on our happiness and blessings, and is a clearing of the mind.

My hope is that you form this journal into whatever you want it to be. More than you even know, you are passionate and imaginative. Now, it's your turn to craft your own book, just like I have. Take whatever is inside your head and all that is in your heart, and turn it into something beautiful.

Stay Strong,

Demi

There is nothing noble in being
superior to your fellow man. True nobility
is being superior to your former self.

—ERNEST HEMINGWAY

Let go or be dragged.

—ZEN PROVERB

The only time you should look in your neighbor's bowl is to make sure that they have enough. You don't look in your neighbor's bowl to see if you have as much as them.

—LOUIS C.K.

Let everything happen to you.
Beauty and terror. Just keep going.
No feeling is final.

—RAINER MARIA RILKE

Write hard and clear about what hurts.

—ERNEST HEMINGWAY

Life has many ways of testing a person's will,
either by having nothing happen at all, or by
having everything happen all at once.

—PAULO COELHO

Take your time, don't live too fast.
Troubles will come and they will pass.

—LYNYRD SKYNYRD, "SIMPLE MAN"

If you don't like where you are, move.
You are not a tree.

—UNKNOWN

Living is a form of not being sure, not knowing
what next or how. . . . We guess. We may be
wrong, but we take leap after leap in the dark.

—AGNES DE MILLE

Believe you can and you're halfway there.

—THEODORE ROOSEVELT

You are confined only by the walls
you build yourself.

—ANDREW MURPHY

I know for sure that what we dwell on
is who we become.

—OPRAH WINFREY

Love yourself first and everything else falls into line.

—LUCILLE BALL

Don't be pushed by your problems.
Be led by your dreams.

—RALPH WALDO EMERSON

Life is a beautiful, magnificent thing,
even to a jellyfish.

—CHARLIE CHAPLIN

Don't give up. Remember, it's always the last key
on the key ring that opens the door.

—PAULO COEHLO

Change your thoughts and you change the world.

—NORMAN VINCENT PEALE

Do the best you can until you
know better. Then when you
know better, do better.

—MAYA ANGELOU

Be you, bravely.

—UNKNOWN

Be silly. Be honest. Be kind.

—RALPH WALDO EMERSON

Honesty will never break you.

—KATE HUDSON

Through every dark night,
there's a bright day after that.

—TUPAC SHAKUR, "ME AGAINST THE WORLD"

Continue to share your heart with
people even if it's been broken.

—AMY POEHLER

Nobody can go back and start a new beginning,
but anyone can start today and make a new ending.

—MARIA ROBINSON

Raise your words, not your voice.
It is rain that grows flowers, not thunder.

—RUMI

Expect nothing. Appreciate everything.

—UNKNOWN

Follow your heart,
but take your brain with you.

—ALFRED ADLER

Two things define you: Your patience when you have nothing, and your attitude when you have everything.

—UNKNOWN

Never give up on a dream just because of the time it will take to accomplish it. The time will pass anyway.

—EARL NIGHTINGALE

Forgiveness is giving up
the hope that the past
could be any different.

—OPRAH WINFREY

When things go wrong, don't go with them.

—ELVIS PRESLEY

Always remember to fall asleep with
a dream and wake up with a purpose.

—UNKNOWN

On the other side of fear lies freedom.

—UNKNOWN

You are more than the mistakes you've made.

—UNKNOWN

Live your life, live your life,
live your life.

—MAURICE SENDAK